Please let me remember this

What I hope my memory keeps

Tahlia Doyle

written and created by Tahlia Doyle
cover design by the author, using original photography

first edition
isbn: 978-1-7647082-0-3

for my children,
for the love you've given me
and the life you've shown me

for my husband,
for the life we've built
and the love that holds it

for my parents,
for the life you gave me
and the love that shaped it

author's note:

these pages were written in real time
in the middle of living them

some were shaped by love
some by waiting
some by moments i didn't yet understand

they are not perfect recollections
but feelings as they were
while they were happening

this book isn't a beginning or an ending
just a collection of moments
i didn't want to forget

i love this life
that holds my whole beating heart,
the thought of leaving
pulls my aching chest apart,
i want tomorrow,
and every story after that,
my children grown,
still running home to where love sat,
grandkids laughing loudly
in warm summer afternoon light,
tiny hands reaching,
generations woven tight,
family photos multiplying
faster than the passing years,
new birthdays, wrinkles,
wisdom, laughter, tears,
i want to witness every chapter,
every heartbreak healed after disaster,
every love story beginning softly,
every child becoming somebody lovely,
because loving them
hurts beautifully,
a fullness too vast sometimes,
it swells beneath my ribs,
until tears fall quietly,
so much love,
still here,
more

the pull

i was looking for you,
yet you found me first,
a love with nothing to quench it,
only an aching, yearning thirst,
as flames moved quietly through my throat,
we stood too close to even note,
a wanted kiss, unspoken still,
the world reduced to quiet will,
and everything i thought i knew
collapsed into the pull of you

emotional balm

let's raise a glass to a love that is patient,
that gently nudges when life turns complacent,
a love that carries both courage and calm,
like steady hands offering emotional balm,
it doesn't rush, it doesn't demand,
it simply stays close, soft in your hand,
reminding the heart when it drifts too far,
that love is still here,
exactly where you are

<h1 style="text-align:center">once the unknown</h1>

you were once the unknown,
now you're my home,
a genuine person,
an honest face,
you help me feel at ease,
in any unfamiliar place,
a steady presence when i drift,
a calm that softly becomes my shift,
from uncertainty into something known,
where i no longer feel alone

a knot of knowing

our bodies rest entwined in a knot of knowing,
your breath against me softens what was once
unshowing,
your heart feels close beneath your rib and
chest,
a steady quiet rhythm that teaches my own to
rest,
my love is woven through every fibre of me,
and still it feels too small for what you make
me see,
you are enough, even when the world says
you're not,
even when doubt tries to rewrite what you've
got,
thank you for everything you've been and
become,
for the way you turn ordinary moments into
home,
to me you are a gift that does not lessen with
time,
but returns again and again like something
divine

where it was quiet

i'd lay back in water so still, it barely felt like
moving,
the sky above, the sand below, and me
somewhere between,
mum on the shore, a shape in the distance,
watching without worry,
the sea would lift, then settle again, until it
reached my ears,
and for a moment, everything would disappear,
just water, and that quiet underneath it,
my heartbeat, slow, steady, mine,
then it would fall away, sound returning softly,
like nothing had happened,
but it had,
because even now, years later, i can find that
place again,
where the world fades out, and all that's left,
is the calm i first felt there

it's funny how when i'm not with you,
i avoid the gaze of others,
their faces feel strange and distant,
and i don't want to read what lingers there,
judgement, sadness, something i can't name,
but when i'm with you i feel whole,
like a light switches on inside me,
one that only shines when you are near,
you are the spark that fuels it,
the pulse that steadies my soul,
the part of me that feels most like me,
and suddenly faces soften,
they become something i want to understand,
to turn each expression into wonder,
or hope, or something kinder,
it's a strange thing,
how two energies side by side
can create something larger than themselves,
something vibrant, full, unrepeatable,
my light,
my life

sharp truth

you make me feel dangerous,
in the best ways i can be,
you pull the veil from over my eyes,
so i can finally see,
the world not as it once disguised,
but as it quietly reflects me back,
a sharper truth,
a clearer line,
where i stop folding into lack,
and in that space,
both raw and new,
i learn what strength can come to be,
not reckless fire,
not chaos made,
but something steady inside of me

the sun appeared that afternoon, and the chill in
the air lingered like a moth to a light,
the air was clean and crisp, the grass fresh
beneath my heels,
the halo of my dress floated just above the stems
of grass,
he stood with confidence, honesty, and the
purest form of love i'd ever laid eyes on,
waiting, steady, as i turned the corner and the
world narrowed into us,
nothing but petals of our history drifting
through the space between,
flowers blooming like they knew what was
coming next,
tunnel vision,
all i saw was him

bound

our young hearts were bound,
when pure devotion was found,
for yesterday, today and tomorrow,
our love grew from the ground,
through soil so deep and profound,
where seeds are buried but still known,
our young hearts were bound,
through sunrise and sundown,
for now, forever and always,
through sun, storms and showers,
like everlasting flowers,
i'll love you in my remaining seconds,
minutes and hours

the perfect combination

they go together like biscuits and milk,
a love so gentle it moves like silk,
with quiet gratitude spoken low,
their devotion runs deeper than they know,
brushstrokes of care across skin and time,
a quiet rhythm, steady and aligned,
together they become something rare,
a living artwork, unforced and bare

the beginning

fingers like laces, loose and entwined,
we sat in the dark as light flickered behind,
clammy palms, a quiet shiver through,
fresh from showers, perfume still new,
a restless leg, a soft tapping beat,
side by side, our arms gently meet,
watching with curiosity, open and bright,
stealing glances when eyes met in flight,
both feeling nervous, excitement and thrill,
this feels like something we'll carry still

hoping and waiting,
loving and hating,
each month an emotion,
as vast as the ocean,
some say to be patient,
your time will soon come,
who knew it would feel this hard,
to become your dad and your mum,
there's a strange weight in wanting so bad,
that even the tears start turning to mad,
feeling so much, yet seeing so little,
each negative makes the strongest hearts brittle

the waiting game

it's a lonely time, this waiting game,
avoiding the clock, though it ticks the same,
no words from family or friends seem to land,
nothing they offer feels quite as it's planned,
they say my emotions are too much to hold,
too heavy, too often, too fractured, too cold,
if you knew what i'm like behind closed doors,
you'd see how the waiting can pull me to floors,
days filled with tears i cannot explain,
as hope and exhaustion keep circling my name,
and still i stand guarded, pretending i'm fine,
protecting the softest and most fragile inside,
as the sun slips away just beyond the hill,
i sit in the quiet and wish for you still,
i know you are somewhere not far out of reach,
but time turns to something i struggle to beat,
and if years keep unfolding as they always have
done,
i hope one day proves i was wrong all along

don't sink

to control is to command,
to stand tall and not fall
into ditches of self-pity and wallow,
when tides begin to roll,
knees deep in the sea,
lift your foot and surge toward the shallow,
exhale for what could have been,
but remember to breathe in the sea air,
for seas are not for many, and most will not dare
to walk their shores
all the way to the edge
on their own

implantation

the aching and tugging i feel within,
a quiet pull beneath the skin,
ignites a light that weeks before was dim,
soft, uncertain, thick and then thin,
the cramp and flutter, the subtle strain,
like distant echoes through my frame,
feeding hope and nervous thought,
on every sign my body's caught,
each wave that comes, then slips away,
keeps me suspended in the grey,
between what's wished and what is true,
and all the things i cannot view,
so i sit with breath and shifting time,
reading each signal like a sign,
holding gently what may be,
this small, uncertain part of me

take it easy, they tell her,
as she stands, flushed, reaching for air,
"take it easy," the echo repeats,
but all the women inside her disagree,
they shake their heads in silent reply,
because easy is not the way this feels,
not in her body, not in her mind, not in truth,
what part of this is easy
when all she can feel is fear,
and still she stands,
holding herself together
through something no one else can see

safe and held

when will my body be ready again,
primed at baseline and most fertile then,
she asks it softly, counting the days,
as time moves forward in uncertain ways,
will it take months, or longer still,
a waiting game against my will,
second time round, will it be kind,
or slower to follow what i have in mind,
i want your home to be fresh and right,
safe in the day and held at night,
so i wait in hope, though fear may creep,
trusting my body knows what to keep

lost

i'm sorry my baby, i choke through tears,
my heart in pieces, held by fears,
you were so strong from the very start,
growing within my hopeful heart,
i held you close, though only inside,
hands on my belly, where you'd hide,
i had such hope my body would know,
how to keep you safe, help you grow,
i'm sorry i couldn't make it be,
what i dreamed about so desperately,
they said the words i couldn't deny,
and still i cannot say goodbye,
i love you more than words can show,
more than i ever thought i'd know,
and if there is a place beyond,
i hope you feel i'm still so fond,
of every second you were mine,
my baby, held outside of time

the one that made it,
fresh, then frozen,
then thawed for me,
our five-cell embaby chosen,
no words or tears could ever say
the love that lived there every day,
you meant more than i can explain,
a quiet hope, a tender pain,
our five-cell embaby,
a part of him, a part of me,
if time allows, if stars align,
i'll hold you in another time

becoming

i remember daydreaming of when you would arrive,
a little embryo in my womb just starting to thrive,
and when that day came, no words could explain,
the rush that flooded my body and brain,
for you were the one who chose us that day,
a quiet kind of miracle in its own way,
a moment suspended, forever kept,
one we return to when the nights feel a stretch,
appointments were many,
emotions ran wide,
yet hope kept returning each time we tried,
we learned how heartbreak can circle and bend,
and still somehow lead you back around again,
then came the call, congratulations she said,
and suddenly silence was spinning my head,
our six celled embryo growing and true,
becoming a promise of me and of you,
tears came fast, i could not disguise,
the way everything softened behind my eyes,
i hurried to gather a secret, a plan,
a small future stitched with my shaking hands,
your dad came home, unaware of the tide,
until i broke open what i had tried to hide,
a newborn outfit, a card, our needles too,
all of it marking what we had been through,
not just pain, but a love that survived,
our journey with you just beginning alive

two tiny hopes

happy, content and ready,
we are to start and take things steady,
an excitement unlike anything i've known,
two tiny hopes from what was sown,
are our embryos boys or girls,
little mysteries in waiting worlds,
i need this chance to go just right,
to hold you close, to hold you tight,
for being your mum has left me raw,
emotional, forgetful, loving more,
yet still i wait with open heart,
for every new beginning to start,
to meet our next sweet angel near,
i carry hope through joy and fear

before you even had a heartbeat,
before i knew your face,
you crossed the room in careful hands,
in silence and in grace,
a tiny life within a needle,
fragile, small, unseen,
yet somehow carrying the weight,
of every hope and dream,
the room was bright and far too cold,
my breath held tight with fear,
watching the smallest flicker move,
while wishing you were here,
and all at once my whole wide world,
became that careful thread,
a whispered wish, a trembling hope,
a future softly led,
you were not born into my arms,
the way some stories start,
you were carried there long before,
first placed inside my heart

two in one

two hearts beating in one body,
so wanted, never chance or surprise,
two hearts beating through aching bones,
through swollen feet and sleepless eyes,
two hearts beating over and over,
counting down till the day you come,
still i cannot quite believe,
you chose me to be your mum,
two hearts and a love so fierce,
you outgrew every dream of mine,
for months you lived beneath my ribs,
your blood becoming part of mine,
and from the moment my body changed,
stretching softly with your form,
i knew your soul would leave its mark,
long before your life was born

this body of mine made magic,
when it held both our hearts inside,
quietly changing, shaping, becoming,
while i learned how to stretch and abide,
this body of mine, it opened and grew,
through every fear i never once knew,
until you arrived and everything shifted,
and suddenly i understood what i'd been lifted to do,
others may notice what time has rewritten,
the lines and the softness, the way i am changed,
but i think of the miracle that lived underneath it,
the way every cell in me quietly arranged,
this body of mine made magic,
not perfect, not easy, but deeply divine,
and when i look at you looking at me,
i know it was always meant to be mine

all that you know

my body has changed,
mind a little deranged,
but to you i am all that you know,
you grew safe by my heart,
here now never apart,
my boy i will always love you so

<h1 style="text-align:center">already loved</h1>

your sweet little face is all that it takes,
to light up my nights and soften my days,
your sweet little nudges and funny little
wriggles,
you're my sun, my moon, my stars and
bright rays,
the twinkle in my tummy, the spark in my
veins,
i can feel your love for me, and mine for
you, an infinite flame,
the warmth in my skin, and the light in my
eyes,
yearning to meet you, and watch you
brighten our lives

the red of love

when i saw him,
my brain had blacked out,
with all the red of love,
blood and cut showing,
the room started slowing,
as they held our baby above

they lifted the curtain, so i could not see,
the way motherhood was being carved into me,
bright hospital light, cold air against trembling skin,
machines humming softly beside the sound of my
heartbeat, and somewhere beyond the sheet,
were the doctors, with their steady hands,
opening my body, like love itself lived underneath it,
and it did,
because then came that impossible moment,
pressure, pulling,
the strange feeling of being emptied and made whole,
all at once, and suddenly,
you were here, my babies,
lifted from beneath my ribs,
like the moon being pulled from the ocean,
wet hair, squinted eyes,
tiny furious cries,
that split the world into,
before you, and after, i never saw the incision, only the
miracle, only the way my chest collapsed inward, the
second i heard your voices, the way tears escaped me
instantly,
as if my soul recognised yours, before my hands even
could,
people speak of fear when they speak of surgery,
but all i remember is magic

even when the spinal didn't work completely,
even when i could still feel pain,
still move my legs,
my feet,
my toes beneath the drapes,
nothing could touch the wonder of that moment,
because how could i focus on anything else,
when the greatest days of my life,
were being placed into my arms,
nothing mattered except you,
not the operating room,
not the fear,
not the discomfort,
just the sound of your cries,
and the overwhelming knowing,
that every hard thing in my life,
had somehow led me exactly here,
and somehow,
there is nothing violent,
about the place my children entered from,
because that scar is not where i was broken,
it is where the universe,
opened me,
wide enough,
to become,
your mother

it was dark outside,
when you cried,
for cuddles, warmth and food,
i'd gather you in my arms, feed and burp you,
until you milky spewed,
and once you were done,
i'd then start to hum,
watching you with eyes of love,
they were such special times,
just you and i,
and the glow from the moon up above

finally it found me

i spent years wondering what my heart searched for,
why joy still felt like it was missing something more,
then suddenly, under bright hospital light,
the whole of my world came rushing into sight,
one cry,
one breath,
one tiny trembling boy,
and somehow my soul recognised him instantly with joy,
the room disappeared when they placed you on my chest,
and for the very first time, life made complete sense,
not partly,
not almost,
not close enough to whole,
but like every broken piece had finally found its role,
your tiny face rewrote the meaning of my name,
and nothing before you ever felt the same,
the ache, the waiting, the fears i carried through,
all softened the second i laid my eyes on you,
because you were never just a baby to hold tight,
you were the answer to every unanswered night,
the reason the hard years never went to waste,
the missing piece my heart had always chased,
and even now, i cannot explain it quite right,
how one little boy could make the whole world bright,
only that before you, life wandered endlessly, and then i
saw your face,
and finally,
it found me

my baby girl,
with features so delicate,
and eyes that felt familiar,
like i had known you before we met,
you did not complete me,
your brother had already shown me,
what impossible love could feel like,
but you deepened it,
you stretched my heart wider than i knew it could go,
until love no longer felt contained,
but endless,
and there was something,
about seeing your dad hold you,
the softness in his face,
the quiet awe,
the way we looked at each other,
and didn't need words,
because there you were,
our girl,
our daughter,
a whole new universe,
in warm skin and sleepy breaths,
and in that moment,
nothing rushed,
nothing hurt,
nothing existed outside that room,
only the knowing,
we had been given something sacred again

i don't recall the loudest days,
just how it felt with you,
an easy kind of laughter there,
that always felt like truth,
you'd tell a story, laugh halfway,
then tell it all again,
the same old lines, the same soft grin,
like comfort never ends,
and even now, just thinking back,
it rises, warm and odd,
that quiet kind of happiness,
we're still just peas in a pod

sweet slumber

i am your soundtrack,
your soundtrack to your rest,
my heartbeat, my warmth, my smell, my hold,
as you surrender upon my chest,
the world falls quiet where we begin,
as sleep pulls softly from within,
and all that matters in this space,
is the calm i find in your tiny face

fuzzy and warm,
in the midst of a storm,
while thunder and lightning clap,
rain starts to pour,
you feel safe and secure,
eyes close as you begin to nap,
nestled right in,
as i stroke your cheek's skin,
my love makes my heart beat double,
no matter the weather or worries in the world,
you're safe in this mummy love bubble

there were three in our bed,
and the little one fed,
while mum and dad lay still,
listening to sleepy breaths,
and tiny milk-filled sighs,
our baby tucked between us,
warm beneath the morning light,
us three together,
before the world arrived

big things

we fall in love with the little things,
the way he tilts his head when he thinks,
the soft scrunch of his nose when he laughs,
we fall in love with the little things,
the warmth of his breath when he sleeps,
the rhythm of his steps on the stairs,
the way his eyebrows lift in surprise,
as the world flickers behind his eyes,
we fall in love with the little things,
the familiar weight of his hands,
the quiet comfort of his presence,
like something we've always known and understood,
we fall in love with the little things,
yet none of them ever feel small,
because together they become everything,
and he becomes the reason for it all

not wonder but knowing

sometimes it's wonder in his eyes,
that takes my breath away by surprise,
i know this world is new for him,
that twinkle in his eye i hope won't dim,
for there is so much more out there,
so many things we will get to share,
for years to come and many more,
those fresh little eyes will explore,
sometimes it's wonder in his eyes,
full of innocence with no disguise,
there is one look that i sometimes see,
not wonder but knowing,
that he loves me

they reach for me,
and i make sure i am always there,
to soften whatever waits,
on the other end of their touch,
he looks at me with wide, excited eyes,
desperate to tell me,
how beautiful the sunset is,
as though he has discovered it himself,
just to share it with me,
and then she copies him,
her tiny hand pointing toward the same sky,
mirroring her big brother,
in the sweetest ways,
both of them looking back at me,
with eyes full of wonder and magic,
like the world is still soft,
still beautiful,
still safe,
because i am in it with them

that smile,
eyes half shut,
teeth on display,
i could sit and admire you every minute of
the day,
nose scrunched up,
head bopping around,
all the noises in the world, your laugh is my
favourite sound,
legs stretched out and tensed in pike,
heaven on earth is what being with you
feels like,
sloppy kisses and little hands squeezing all,
i wish my baby could stay forever this small

milky breath and tiny toes,
chubby thighs and cheeks soft rose,
curled lashes and sweet pursed lips,
dimply knees and dribble that drips,
soft fresh skin and feathered hair,
when my baby sleeps i lovingly stare,
every sigh and sleepy sound,
feels like magic wrapped and found,
and in the quiet stillness there,
nothing on earth could ever compare

the light pours,
as he snores,
through the glass above me,
he is happy,
we are happy,
tell me sun,
is that what,
you see,
do you watch us in quiet ease,
as life settles into these soft routines,
do you notice the way love lives,
not in grand things,
but in simple scenes,
in warm breath,
and resting eyes,
and a home that no longer needs disguise,
if you are looking down at all,
then stay a while,
and let it fall,
because this is all i need to be,
enough for him,
and enough for me

every version of you

i want to remember your faces,
not only as they are today,
but every version time once cradled,
before it slipped away,
back to that tiny silhouette,
soft flickers on the screen,
the first time that i saw you,
and knew what love could mean,
the curve of cheeks to pursed pink lips,
your little dimpled chin,
the way your features somehow hold,
the souls you carry in,
i want to keep each special freckle safe,
each eyelash sigh and smile,
the way your sleepy eyes looked up,
and made my world worthwhile,
because one day these little hands i hold,
will reach and find just air,
and all i'll have are memories,
of who you once were there,
so let me burn these moments deep,
where time cannot be cruel,
your faces pressed inside my heart,
forever mine and beautiful

time may keep on moving

hard times awake, watching night turn
into day,
the weeks and months will fly on by, so
soak it up they say,
i know this is the reason for the pull
that tugs my heart,
the ache of loving something time can
never pause or part,
because days move quickly, even when
we beg them slow,
tiny hands grow steadier, little voices
deeper as they grow,
but no matter how fast the years rush
past and depart,
time may keep on moving,
but it will never tear us apart

w h a t   w e   k e e p

as the days creep into weeks,
into months, then a year has passed,
i hope and wish for every moment of the day,
that this bond, this breath, this magic lasts,
each piece of time i hold and save,
like something precious, quiet, brave,
i wonder which moments you will keep,
when memory grows tall and deep,
as you grow and change and time moves on,
softly rewriting what once felt strong,
oh these days, these weeks, these months,
how quickly they arrive and then are gone

50

and in this world right now i say,
they are my world for forever and a day,
the centre of every hope i keep,
the reason love runs endlessly deep,
and if time should shift and seasons stray,
my heart will still belong to them,
forever and a day

the sky is on fire,
with colours i desire,
as daylight loosens its hold,
the sky starts to burn,
and the whole world turns,
to watch the horizon unfold,
gold spills into embered red,
like thoughts we never said,
and blue slips quietly away,
the sky takes the stage,
in a slow blazing rage,
that no one could ever delay,
it demands every eye,
without needing to try,
as silence grows thick in the air,
and beauty so near,
feels almost unreal,
pulling attention everywhere,
then it softens and fades,
through its flame coloured shades,
as night learns to follow its cue,
and i stand underneath,
with a still kind of breath,
completely undone by its view

light finds her

amongst the ferns,
is where she learns,
that sunlight can dance and shimmer,
as the clouds start to part,
giving the sun a head start,
and the moon begins to look dimmer,
cross legged on the ground,
with autumn leaves that have browned,
she sits with her face to the bright sky,
thoughts of gold cross her mind, as she exhales a sigh,
thoughts that until now, had stayed quiet and shy

the sea knew first

like a shell,
the ocean smoothed me,
softening my edges with the pull of the sea,
wave after wave it shaped what i'd been,
washing away the sharpness hidden within,
and when i finally felt whole enough,
ready to rise and speak up loud,
the ocean roared against the shore,
as though it had always known i could,
and clapped for the person i'd become,
so fierce and proud

the wind, it licks my skin to taste,
the sun, it danced, beams i would chase,
the shade, it hovered above me tall,
the snow was shy, it'd barely fall,
the rain would drip down on my arm,
the sky would roar, then silence with calm,
an unforgiving shift of mood and light,
yet comfort lingered in its sight,
no matter storm or golden hue,
the sky still held me coming through

when night arrives,
my stomach turns,
to trembling static beneath,
where time and life and all i am,
feel fragile underneath,
i lie with heavy, aching arms,
pressed deep into the bed,
while anxious fingers brush stray hairs,
from spiralling thoughts unsaid,
and in the dark,
the dread appears,
soft grief i cannot name,
for passing years and fleeting moments,
that never stay the same,
i mourn the times not yet gone,
the ones i'll someday miss,
and fear becomes a tightening ache,
i cannot coexist with,
so i command my mind to stop,
to turn to disappear,
afraid that if i think it long,
i'll somehow pull it near,
because my heart believes at night,
thoughts carry weight somehow,
as if the mind could summon loss,
before its rightful hour

shameful thoughts through a night
of darkness,
stillness suspended in the air
around,
noises of creatures moving in
distance,
life in its quietest form of sound,
far-off rustles, unseen and shifting,
echoes of things that never stay,
even the human world feels like
wilderness,
when silence refuses to turn away,
and in that hush where nothing
answers back,
the mind grows loud in its own
accord,
yet somewhere beyond the weight of
thinking,
the night keeps breathing, wordless,
toward dawn

the air shifts softly through the room,
i wonder if even it can sense the doom,
feelings are said to float unseen,
yet here they press through every seam,
"i can feel it in the air," we say,
when something shifts but won't give way,
this weight is not loud, not sharp, not fast,
but settles in corners where calm won't last,
it lingers in silence, in half-closed doors,
in the pause before footsteps cross the floors,
doom moves like something just out of sight,
a leaning shadow that steals the light,
a presence that follows without a sound,
until even your thoughts feel tightly wound,
and where it settles, gloom draws near,
turning breath into something you feel more
than hear,
until the room feels smaller than it should,
and even breathing doesn't feel as it could

where calm once was

eyes turn wide,
as senses collide and heighten,
the world grows sharp and suddenly tightens,
my body locks still, completely frozen,
caught in a moment i never had chosen,
my breath turns quick, my heartbeat thumping,
panic erupts like a storm system pumping,
blood rushes loud like rivers unbound,
drowning the silence that once was around,
i feel like i'm last in a world left behind,
with seconds that fracture and blur in my mind,
counting it down, what was i worth,
as fear fills the space where there once was calm
earth

the storm within

at times i sit in a silence of pain,
as my mind brews a storm with words like
rain,
heavy drops of insult, currents of shame,
pour over my spirit and call out my name,
the water keeps rising, the flooding won't
stop,
and confidence crumbles where dark
thoughts drop,
my chest feels heavy, my breathing turns
thin,
as the storm outside quiets, but roars
within,
so i sit in the silence and drown in its
stream,
for my mind is a torrent, cruelly of me,
and no matter how hard i fight to stay
above,
self hatred feels louder than reason or love

teeth in the quiet

sometimes i push them down,
other times i bottle them up,
a crease crosses my face,
a quiet sign i've had enough,
sometimes i bury them deep,
sometimes i stand under water and weep,
sometimes they're meant to be shared,
other times secrets i choose to keep,
some say they'd gladly take them,
others say they wish they could trade,
but they don't understand the weight they carry
or the silence they've made,
if they stay in my head too long,
they don't stay thoughts at all,
they grow teeth in the quiet
and turn everything inside me small

is she alone

is she alone,
i often ask myself,
wondering if those around me
place our friendship on the top shelf,
some may care and others may not,
yet still the question returns more than it ought,
in my mind, where everything unthreads,
where doubt and silence fill my head,
i sift through echoes of what i've been shown,
and answer myself in a voice of my own,
for it has always felt this way,
yes, she's alone,
i let my voice say

the loudest voice

queasy and ill,
i can't keep my hands still,
cracking, kneading, and picking,
dry in my mouth,
damp skin all around,
it feels like my patience is ticking,
housebound and tired,
yet somehow still wired,
no conversations i want said aloud,
my muscles feel heavy,
i'm not yet ready
to say that for this i am proud,
with nothing to say
and nothing to be said,
how can my voice be the loudest
inside my own head

this into that

i thought it was this,
but it turned into that,
long conversations
faded into chit chat,
who would have known
until actions were shown,
that being your friend
was something i'd outgrow

truth on the tongue

give me a moment,
while i pull the thorns from my tongue,
before i speak the truths she once sung,
where caution became the only way
to speak without pain, or so they would say,
every word measured carefully,
trimmed down soft and small,
because honesty in the wrong hands
could feel like a fall,
so now i stand unlearning silence,
slowly undoing what fear has done,
teaching my mouth that truth was never meant
to hurt this much on the tongue

shock and wince,
he's hard to convince,
when listening he doesn't hear,
repeating and waiting,
silence makes it frustrating,
for my words are said loud and clear,
"are you even listening" i question,
he stares with no expression,
how odd someone can be,
if words are not working,
then my tears would be irking,
someone with eyes to see me

checking

there were rules inside our heads
that nobody else could hear,
small compulsions circling endlessly,
fed quietly by fear,
the checking locks, the counting steps,
the "just once more" again,
the awful weight of knowing
you cannot trust your own mind,
you'd turn the car around sometimes
just to make sure things were right,
and i would replay conversations
for hours every night,
and how do you explain to people
who've never felt that dread,
what it's like to fear your own thoughts
more than anything ahead,
to know it makes no sense at all
yet still feel terror rise,
your heart reacting to imagined grief
like it's already arrived

h a p p i n e s s   i n - b e t w e e n

happiness is there,
not just in your heart, but behind your eyes,
though your mind insists you're not,
as your spine slumps with restless sighs,
it speaks in noise, in doubt and lies,
turning small thoughts into towering skies,
but beneath it all, just out of sight,
there is a quieter truth, held light,
because happiness isn't always loud or seen,
it's often still there,
in-between

how love becomes responsibility,
how danger hides in air,
how your mind convinces you
that safety rests within your care,
so we lived exhausted, quietly,
pretending we were fine,
while carrying invisible alarms
that never stopped in time,
and the cruelest part of all of it
was looking so composed,
while panic bloomed like wildfire
behind the lives we showed,
two people smiling normally,
while somewhere deep inside,
our minds were pulling fire alarms
no one else could hear at night

instructions for becoming

make this smaller,
grow a little taller,
cut your hair just right,
make the fat disappear,
walk like this,
talk like that,
be confident,
but not a brat,
don't wear makeup,
just a little there,
make eye contact,
but don't you dare stare,
don't exercise too much,
but get leaner each day,
smile and nod
when you don't know what to say,
be her, be me,
do all the work,
no guarantee,
your body's the problem,
fix it, conceal,
moderation is key,
these people aren't real

what did i say, or how did i say it,
i got up and left, feeling too sick to stay
in it,
was it my tone, should i have laughed it
away,
now regret sits heavy and won't fade
away,
second guessing every sentence i let slip,
words turning clumsy as they fell from
my lips,
the rest of them speak like it flows into
song,
effortless, polished, like nothing is
wrong,
while i replay each fragment i tried to
release,
as it rushed out in nerves i couldn't quite
piece,
every line i revisit, i pull it apart,
like i'm searching for proof i was wrong
from the start,
and it lingers, it lingers, that moment in
time,
where i question each word i once
thought was mine

a friend like her

a friend by my side through thick and thin,
always there to make me laugh and make me grin,
she's held my hand through quiet days,
and sat with me in tea-filled haze,
i call her friend, but truth runs deep,
she's more like sister i get to keep,
a sister with no hidden cost,
nothing gained and nothing lost,
she stays through joy, she stays through pain,
through sunlit days and heavy rain,
when i feel lost, or small, or bare,
she answers still, she's always there,
she says she's lucky we align,
but i feel luck has been all mine,
she makes me laugh until i cry,
and lifts me up when i'm too shy,
so thank you for each year we've grown,
for every memory we've known,
we've got a lifetime left ahead,
and i'll walk it with you, like i said

i watered gardens with careful hands,
pulled every weed,
tended the lands,
but some flowers only learn to take,
drinking deeply,
giving nothing back

the sky still wakes

when they shout the world will end,
i do not fear it, my voice will defend,
for the world has ended many times before,
inside grieving hearts and behind closed doors,
and still the morning finds its way,
returning softly with each new day,
with sunlight spilling across the floor,
and hope knocking gently at the door,
i have survived too many endings now
to fear each warning spoken aloud,
because even after ruin and ache,
the earth still turns,
and the sky still wakes

like nothing else

no interest elsewhere,
nothing could compare,
to the love i hold for you,
connected from the start,
two ever-beating hearts,
in something lasting, strong and true

on your way home

just be patient,
take your time,
you are already on your way home,
and home is not a place you find,
but something carried in your heart and mind,
a quiet knowing beneath the noise,
a softness waiting beyond the void,
so move gently through what you cannot yet see,
for the person you are becoming
is already reaching for you

i walk at someone else's pace,
learning to take each day as it comes,
the passing weeks are not a race,
and time is not something i need to outrun,
some days i stumble, some i stand,
finding my rhythm as life shifts its hand,
and even as the world moves fast,
i remind myself this too will pass,
there is no prize in rushing through,
only the quiet work of becoming you

you will laugh again,
as life loosens what it once held tight,
you will find your rhythm again
in the quiet return of day and night,
hope will come back in softer ways,
not all at once, but enough to stay,
and piece by piece, without demand,
you'll recognise yourself where you stand,
not as someone lost or far from whole,
but as someone rebuilding a steady soul,
because even after all you've been through,
you don't disappear,
you come back through you

a beginning written in light

you were born
when the sun lay low,
peeking through rusted leaves below,
when the air was crisp and softly still,
and water held its glass-like chill,
you were here,
a beginning written in light,
a whisper forming into life,
an unfinished line, yet already whole,
a quiet marking on the soul,
you were born,
and everything leaned in close,
as if the world already chose
to pause, to watch, to simply know
this moment would not let you go

for me to fall asleep,
i replay the words you said,
like echoes moving softly
through the corners of my head,
they loop through every silence
where the day has come undone,
and linger in the darkness
long after night has won,
and somewhere in that repetition
my thoughts begin to slow,
as if your voice becomes the place
i finally let myself go

twelve months of us

a year has come and gone,
a whole year since you were born,
a year i swore i would savour,
a year with the one i adore,
twelve months of becoming, of learning your name,
of soft little moments that never feel the same,
each day a reminder, each night held in view,
that time keeps on moving, but i move with you,
every small change, every laugh, every start,
another deep carving into my heart,
a year i will keep, not let slip from my sight,
a year made of love, and of holding you tight

him and he,
are all that i need,
in this world of us,
him and he,
all i hoped it could be,
anyone else just a plus,
a quiet world where love feels enough,
simple, steady, unshaken stuff,
where every moment finds its place,
in the calm of his familiar face

my spring time

spring comes when i'm in your arms,
against your heart and soul,
i bloom into my truest self,
like something gently made whole,
the seasons soften around me there,
where all my guarded pieces slow,
and in the quiet of your presence,
i become someone softer to know

the warmth you'll know

every sunset feels sacred now,
like something soft and true,
as though the ones we ache for most
still shine their light straight through,
i stand beneath the painted sky
and hold them in my mind,
the people love could never keep
but time could never bind,
and when the clouds turn gold and pink,
i hope you'll always pause,
to feel how beauty still survives
despite the grief it caused,
because one day i'll leave here too,
far past what eyes can see,
and i hope sunsets will become
a quiet place for me,
i hope the warmth upon your skin
will feel a little known,
like somewhere in the evening light
a piece of me comes home

i wish the ink would scrawl and write,
just the way i think,
obsessively,
compulsively,
a thousand words before one blink,
i'd write with a hunger so insatiable,
that suffocation felt the only way to stop,
as i put my pen to paper,
no letters arrive as ink would start to drop,
i'd write so ferociously,
that sentences formed with ease,
jotting down each graphic image,
into words made from mental disease,
i wish the ink would scrawl and write,
just the way i think,
if written words could satisfy the parch,
i'd have nothing left to drink

petal and grit

entwined and enchanting,
grown over planting,
spreading like love with petal and stem,
raw on the edges,
soft in the mid,
between rocks, pavers and bricks laid in grid,
the hardness surrounding,
allows growth so compounding,
blooming with colour, leaf and grit,
resilient and adaptive,
soft but secure,
in times of darkness,
creates a light so pure,
there every moment,
loving every hour,
who knows the strength it takes,
to grow like a wildflower,
forever changing and going with earth's flow,
surrendering with no question,
a mother would know

it got in anyway

no doors knocked, no bells rang,
"you're not normal," my conscience sang,
no footsteps outside, no warning at all,
it slipped right in and stood over me tall,
no small talk, no smiles, no time to prepare,
if i'd known it was coming i'd have fled anywhere,
that familiar feeling, a wave i detest,
that heavy, crushing weight on my chest,
my stomach turns for what's yet to come,
it rushes toward me, my heart like a drum,
it's here now, present, making itself known,
slipping through cracks no lock could have shown,
no barrier held it, no sound to give out,
a silence that swallows my scream and my shout,
it fills up the air my lungs try to steal,
my body gives way as i drop and i kneel,
no thought to surrender, no will in the act,
just something inside me tightening its grasp,
my mind overtaken, no space left intact,
this is depression, and that is a fact

magic is simply her

some don't believe in
magic,
no imagination to soften
what feels tragic,
"you have to see it to
believe it," they say,
but full of love, i smile
and answer their way,
that magic isn't
something you chase or
uncover,
magic is simply
her

the ocean is asking you to come and play,
with each wave that reaches further each
day,
it begins with gentle, pulling yearning,
then shifts to something stronger,
discerning,
the ocean is calling you back to its sway,
each wave an outstretched hand that won't
go away,
but the ocean can turn when the winds
grow rough,
and fall into stillness when enough is
enough,
its calm arrives without warning or say,
yet it has taken many and carried them
away,
still the ocean asks you to come and play,
kissing the sand with shells and spray,
it longs for laughter, for company, for joy,
but a temper like the ocean's can quickly
destroy,
and if you surrender to all it can show,
the ocean will keep you and not let you go

close your eyes but leave the light,
something is given in the quiet of night,
the moon shares its glow with the bulbs in
your room,
as you lie wrapped deep in your blanket
cocoon,
someone is taken in the silence of night,
when thoughts grow heavy and nothing feels
right,
loneliness drifts through the sheets meant for
protection,
whispering softly of lost direction,
so close your eyes but leave the light,
when the night takes hold, you'll be alright,
and think of them smiling when darkness
feels tight

chattering afar, a sound in the distance,
a smile creeps in, laughter in assistance,
how happiness falls on fires of sadness,
yet flooding and ash can blur into
madness,
as wet ground gives way, unsure where to
tread,
and burnt earth still cracks, remembering
the dead,
what lies beneath us can test what we
trust,
as voices around us dissolve into gusts,
and still in the noise where confusion is
spun,
we learn to tell wind apart from the sun

atop a mountain peak,
hold out your fingers and sweep them across the
sky,
lift your arms and stretch your hands before your
eyes,
for wisdom rests lightly across your shoulders,
you can move mountains, split valleys, roll
boulders,
with a strength buried deep in your blood and
bone,
steady in pace, resilient in tone,
while others see the world through softened
glass,
you see every fracture, every impasse,
a reminder that truth can still be freeing,
an enigma of a person, a singular being,
so lose yourself high where the mountains meet
thought,
because minds like yours cannot be purchased or
taught,
think of the in-betweens, the unseen, the unsure,
for truth is rarely comfort, and never born pure

my heart holds so many parts
of you,
so many pieces this love grew
into,
it no longer feels like only
mine,
but something shared,
something intertwined,
it feels wide enough for both of
us,
for all you are, and all you've
become

the weight of ache

the ache in your head,
is your mind being fed
lies and threads of false hope,
the ache in your heart
is what tears you apart
when you're trying to cope,
the ache in your bones
is the weight of old tones
of a life fully lived and once held,
the need to be liked, to be heard, to be known,
before time softens the edges that swelled,
but even through ache, there is something that stays,
a quiet persistence that carries your days,
not everything broken is all that it seems,
some pain is just proof that you're still between dreams

what was taken

we sit and feel this pain together,
quiet in our knowing of one another,
we always knew grief would be the cost
of loving something that could be lost,
and still we carry this burning ache,
a love no ending could ever take,
people say time softens what's left,
but i have learned it is death that is the
thief,
we go on living, though they are gone,
holding them close as we carry on,
hoping they've found a place of peace,
while somehow they never fully leave

you haven't yet lived through the worst
days to come,
or felt the best ones, or weeks gone
numb,
a day is a moment, scattered in time,
a life is a loaf, cut through with good and
grime,
you're shaped and reshaped, pulled apart,
then gathered again, piece by piece, part by
part,
presented to the world to be chosen or
left,
some reaching with care, some taking with
theft,
but no matter the hands that reach for
your bread,
it matters you keep surviving,
and remember to keep your soul fed

alone, but hers

she was the one
who chose to be alone,
and in that choosing
found something of her own,
what once felt empty
slowly shaped into purpose,
something she could hold
instead of simply endure,
and so she held it closely,
with quiet devotion and care,
working toward a life
that finally felt like hers to share

you lived half inside of dreaming, half somewhere i couldn't
see,
speaking softly in your sleep like another version beside
me,
some nights your footsteps filled the hall, small shadows in
the dark,
while the whole house stayed asleep and only i heard your
spark,
and once you shook me half awake, eyes shining wild with
bliss,
whispering "wake up, it's christmas," though it wasn't
anywhere near it,
and somehow for those few minutes the whole world felt
brand new,
because magic always sounded real when it was spoken by
you,
you'd come back clutching tortillas like treasures thieves
had found,
and we'd eat them underneath my bed, careful not to make
a sound,
lying there full of laughter, breath held tight in the night,
as though happiness itself had slipped quietly inside,
and now i think the hardest grief is not the grand goodbye,
but missing tiny sacred things that never learned to survive,
like hearing your voice through bedroom walls or waiting
for your feet,
or wondering if somewhere deep inside you still wander in
your sleep

when i was small

i used to sit so quietly,
just watching you exist,
highlighters staining your hands,
as you studied like the world could shift,
i'd follow the sound of weights downstairs,
the rhythm of your shoes,
pretending not to hover close,
just to spend time near you,
and even when she sat beside you,
the girl who'd be your wife,
you never made me feel too small
to still belong inside your life,
but what i remember most of all
is every time you'd stand,
between me and the kind of hurt
only brothers understand,
you'd say my name like it mattered,
like i deserved protecting too,
and suddenly i wasn't outnumbered anymore,
because i still had you,
and maybe you never realised
what those moments made me feel,
but to a little girl with two big brothers,
your kindness felt unreal,
like i was something worth defending,
something steady, safe, and known,
like gold held carefully in sunlight,
instead of being left alone

99

the moment we met you

your happiness is all i need on this earth,
i knew that long before your birth,
from the moment we realised we had made
you one,
our whole world felt like it had just begun,
you gave us strength, a deeper kind of pride,
to carry each day knowing you were inside,
and when we saw you, lifted into view,
something in us shifted, something we always
knew,
your arrival wasn't just a dream come true,
it rewrote everything we thought we knew,
you became our everything, quiet and fast,
a love that settled,
and was always meant to last

<h1 style="text-align:center">my favourite subject</h1>

a subject so adored,
i would paint you a thousand times and still not be
done,
you linger behind every thought i've ever spun,
a presence so constant, so quietly bright,
i'd trace you into silence on a cold, empty night,
not out of absence, not out of need,
but because you are the image my thoughts always
lead,
and if i were to write you into language at all,
it would be just to hear your name fall,
soft and certain, spoken in delight,
like love made visible,
in sound and in sight

she felt anxiety
like something dancing on a ledge,
balancing between reason and dread,
as though one wrong thought could pull
her over the edge,
it lingered quietly behind her eyes,
waiting for silence to grow too deep,
turning ordinary moments fragile,
and rest into something she could not
keep

finding it within

it's like someone spiked her drink,
with grit, determination and drive,
just one sip she swallowed that time,
and suddenly she remembered how to feel alive,
no more stumbling through hallways,
reaching for edges in the dark,
no more hands searching walls,
that never answered back,
she walks the corridors of life now,
with a quieter spark,
still learning, still shaking,
but no longer off track,
that drink wasn't magic,
it was something she found,
buried beneath doubt,
beneath all that held her down,
and now that it's gone,
she refuses to forget,
the way it felt to choose herself,
without regret,
so she carries it forward,
not as something she can taste,
but as fire in her bones,
she refuses to waste,
the mission is simple,
though it aches when it's said,
to start truly living,
before the mind turns instead

try to slip away through the crack behind
the bed,
behind where the mattress begins and the
window hangs above your head,
slip away down into the crevice of comfort
and seclusion,
where the room you lie in feels so real it
blurs into illusion,
try to slide on down backwards and slow,
into the quiet that only hidden places know,
to a space where the world cannot follow or
intrude,
where silence feels safe and solitude feels like
food,
to a place where your mind and your soul
are allowed to breathe,
beyond the weight of what you're told to
believe,
where you are more than appearance or
name,
and peace is no longer something you have
to claim

love does not break you

love isn't meant to hurt you,
it will take your mind for a drive,
and keep you out cruising past curfew,
where even fear feels more alive,
love isn't made to take pieces away,
it doesn't leave you less than before,
it stretches the heart in ways it can stay,
and opens up every locked door,
it doesn't demand you to shrink or to hide,
but asks you to meet it halfway inside,
and tell your own mind it can stay,
where love doesn't break you,
it builds you that way

light and lifted, feeling content but weary,
a day out with friends left me soft, bright and bleary,
a slower pace settled in for the night,
conversations replaying when out of sight,
driving back home with my palm to cheek,
a good kind of friendship is something we seek,
once it is found it is always well kept,
a bond that is built, a mutual respect,
arrival to home, a place meant for comfort,
but home is not you, not comforting or observant,
feelings are freed but not always caught here,
sitting in this space wishing true home was near

choose yourself

put yourself first,
feel the crack and the burst
as something shifts and opens in you,
it's time to decide,
to quiet the divide
between what you feel and what you knew,
no longer placing
yourself last in line,
not maybe, not someday, not next,
but choosing the space
where your own life can breathe,
where your heart is no longer suppressed,
and learning that self is not something to lose,
but the one thing you never refuse

they are in the wind

she walks with no purpose,
drenched in morning sun,
guided by a subtle breeze,
she remembers her loved one,
may memories of them fill her
as leaves brush softly at her hands,
pulled by gust and quiet light,
she begins to understand,
her strides begin to quicken,
her thoughts grow calm and clear,
the weight she carried loosens
as she feels her loved one near

he is our heart

i spend each moment looking at him,
as if the world has narrowed to this one truth,
being here, in the same breath of existence,
feels like something i was always meant to reach,
nothing on earth could feel grim
when he is here, unfolding into himself,
so perfectly wild,
so entirely his own,
a dream i once only dared to imagine,
now breathing in front of me,
he is our child,
and still somehow more than that,
he is our heart,
and we are his home

peace is made, not given

she loves life,
just not everything in it,
she hoped she had enough within her,
to make changes and live without limit,
to outgrow the fear that once held her still,
to choose herself fully with courage and will,
because loving life sometimes means learning this truth,
that peace does not arrive,
you build it from ruin and proof

let the mask fall

fight for yourself,
instead of against,
in a world that feels heavy with sadness and angst,
not with force that fractures,
but with strength that restores,
choosing yourself when everything asks for more,
if you can't do just that,
take off your mask still intact,
let it fall, let it breathe, let it crack,
and start filling your life with what it had lacked,
not as someone rebuilt to be small,
but as someone who finally answers their call

"move swiftly," it flickered,
neon humming against the dark,
a command more than a suggestion,
glowing where hesitation once was,
she reached for it, or maybe it reached for her,
and something shattered in the exchange,
light spilling louder than it should,
headlines forming from the fragments,
arrows pulsing, colours calling,
voices rising from electric walls,
"it's time," they said,
"it's yours," they said,
and still she felt herself slipping,
hands grasping at passing moments,
none of them solid enough to hold,
the ground no longer steady beneath her,
only motion, only noise,
and above it all, that same relentless glow,
the one that once felt like direction,
now burning without mercy,
demanding more than she could give,
until somewhere in the rush,
in the blur of becoming and being seen,
she lost the quiet part of herself,
the part that knew how to stay,
how to soften,
how to live

this moment is mine

i dread the day i think this is like
deja vu,
when you're grown and i catch a
glimpse of baby you,
so let me be selfish and hold on a
little too tight,
and live inside this moment like it's
my right,
please let me just love you,
the way that i need to

and when you least expect it,
your world will begin to fracture,
not loudly,
but in the quiet places you forgot to protect,
and from that tremor deep in your bones,
you'll realise how easily certainty dissolves,
how quickly the ground of self becomes unsure,
you'll reach outward,
not to take,
but to steady what remains,
as if giving could anchor you to something
unshakable,
because taking carries a weight you only learn in
hindsight,
it leaves a hollow echo,
a loneliness shaped by what does not return,
and slowly, you begin to understand,
not as a rule,
but as something unfolding within you,
that giving is not loss,
it is the only way you remain whole enough,
to stay standing,
when everything else begins to move

a subject so adored,
i would paint you in a million different ways,
trace your form through shifting light
and carry you across my days,
a subject so pure, so honest, so right,
i'd follow you into the coldest night,
not out of longing, not out of need,
but because you are the only image
my heart has ever agreed,
and if i were to write you into words,
they would fall like quiet sight,
and reading them back to myself
would feel like love made right

at times i sit in a silence of pain,
as my mind brews storms that fall
like rain,
heavy drops of insult, surges of
shame,
crashing down over self esteem and
name,
until the water keeps rising and won't
let go,
and confidence drowns in the
undertow,
so i sit in that silence and drift
through its stream,
my mind just a torrent of self-made
dream

what did i say, better yet how did i say
it,
i got up and left, feeling so sick i
couldn't sit,
was it my tone, should i have laughed a
little more,
whatever i did say has regret planted in
my core,
second guesses about sentences made of
messes,
and words that land too sharp or fall
too flat,
while others speak in effortless rhythm,
like every room already knows where
they're at,
i replay every word my mouth let go,
the way they stumbled out too fast, too
low,
and i keep returning to the moment i
left,
searching for a version that felt less
wrong than that

i remember wondering, will we be a
lucky pair,
would we ever hold a love we'd share,
a baby made of him and i,
his arms around me when i would cry,
he'd whisper softly, we will, just wait,
while hope and fear would sit with
fate,
i often wondered if they knew,
how careless questions cut straight
through,
how every announcement echoed
slow,
like salt pressed gently into what we
didn't show,
rooms we sat in, quiet and small,
smiling politely through it all,
we were once the ones left behind,
watching others live what we could
only hold in mind,
but here we are, on the other side,
and still that road lives deep inside

hard times awake, watching night
turn into day,
weeks and months slip quietly away,
they tell me to savour it, hold it in
view,
as if time listens to anything we do,
but i know this ache, this pull in my
chest,
comes from loving something i
cannot arrest,
because no matter how quickly the
years depart,
time may keep moving,
but it will never take you from my
heart

i learned love before i knew the word for it,
before i could name the warmth at the heart of it,
it was in the hallway,
where i sat cross-legged on the floor each day,
watching you do your hair and makeup there,
powder and brush with such loving care,
lipstick, light, the way you shone,
as if beauty simply lived where you'd gone,
i wondered how your hands just knew,
where everything belonged, as if born to do,
and if mine ever would one day,
when i was old enough to find my way,
to be beautiful too in those same sweet ways,
like watching you in those childhood days,
it was at the kitchen bench, warm and cool,
on stolen mornings home from school,
the old milkshake maker would rattle with cheer,
a sound that still feels close and near,
toast browning slow in the morning sun,
tuna and onion, simple things done,
your ordinary hands, so gentle and smart,
turned hunger to comfort, art to heart,
you made it look easy, never hard,
love served daily without guard,
it was in the dark, too,
small feet padding the hallway through

my bad dreams still clinging tight,
you waking softly in the night,
to find me standing, scared and small,
and somehow making room for all,
for monsters, blankets, fear, and me,
you made the dark feel kind and free,
it was in the mornings, soft and bright,
when laughter filled your bed with light,
me half hanging off the edge,
with joy so big it had no ledge,
my cheeks would ache from laughing through,
the safest place being close to you,
the world stayed far, the day could wait,
your arms made every moment great,
it was in sickness, pale and sore,
when i could not be strong anymore,
the back of your cool hand on my head,
pressed softly where my fever spread,
a touch that said what words never could do,
i am here, and i've got you,
it was in happiness too,
when i had done something well and true,
you never hid your joy away,
you let it shine in the biggest way,
you'd beam so brightly, clap with pride,
cheer so loud with eyes open wide,
and make me feel, in that moment new,
like the whole world celebrated too

it was in sorrow, heavy and slow,
when life had dealt a harder blow,
my head in your lap, quiet there,
your fingers moving through my hair,
with the patience of sunlight, warm and rough,
untangling more than knots enough,
smoothing the places life made tough,
until i felt whole and soft enough,
and now i know,
this is how you learned love so,
not from mirrors,
or recipes,
or passing years,
you learned it by being a mother true,
by giving your whole self the way you do,
and now that i am one too,
i understand more deeply you,
the language of your love so pure,
in ways i never knew before,
i learned it all intensely, so true,
by being loved so heartfelt by you

to be not just a person to someone,
or someone's person,
but to be a place for them,
a place they know is home,
the look, the feel, the smell, all of it,
a home that becomes their favourite spot,
in the whole world,
to be loved and adored so fiercely by two little babies,
and to love them back more than words could ever explain,
is a feeling i longed for, long before i had my babies,
this love is unlike anything else you've ever felt or witnessed,
it feels like heaven on earth,
and i never want it to end,
i want this kind of love,
this joy, pride and soul filling happiness,
to linger day and night,
until the end of eternity,
surely that isn't much to ask,
to you,
i am your person,
your best friend,
your place,
your home,
to me,
you two are my everything,
two pieces of my heart,
living right in front of my eyes

all fire and softness

her laughter finds me before it's sound,
a quiet shift the air has found,
i watch her move, so unaware,
of how i break just standing there,
there are pieces i didn't know were gone,
now living in her, carried on,
stubborn and steady, then soft without warning,
my golden girl, dusk wrapped gently in morning

she moves like she's always known,
exactly where her feet should land,
no second guessing in her bones,
just quiet certainty in her hands,
i see myself in flickers there,
in stubborn steps and steady stare,
his softness too, our son's wild grin,
all of us there in her skin,
and still she stands so wholly sure,
not shaped by doubt or needing more,
a knowing i can't teach or guide,
just something she was born inside

when i'm a man, mama

"when i'm a man," he says,
"i'll buy you a jacket so you're never cold again, okay,
i'll get you a green car just for you, mama,
because it's your favourite colour, so that's what i'll say,
i'll take you everywhere, you can sit with me,
i'll carry you close like you carry me,
i'll bring you flowers on all your days,
and bake you cakes in a hundred ways,
i'll make you smile, i'll make you proud,
i'll love you gently, i'll say it out loud,
wouldn't that make you happy, mama,
when i'm a man, just wait and see"

time will fold

i dread the day i'll think,
this feels like déjà vu,
when you are grown and i catch a glimpse,
of the baby still living inside of you,
a certain smile,
a sleepy stare,
the way you laugh without a care,
and suddenly time will fold in two,
bringing me back to the smallest version of you,
so let me be selfish and relish this time,
as though one day it may feel taboo,
please let me hold you a little longer,
and love you the way i need to

it comes back

you will laugh again,
you will find your rhythm and routine again,
you will feel hope returning through you,
and you will meet yourself again inside you

she writes from the quiet in-between moments,
the ones that often go unnoticed
but hold the most meaning.

her words are shaped by love,
by waiting,
by becoming,
and by the small, fleeting details of everyday life.

this collection is a reflection of those seasons -
of longing and holding,
of breaking and rebuilding,
of learning to sit with both joy and ache at once.

for my children,
you are the reason these words exist at all.
you are my light, my softness, and my forever.

for my husband,
thank you for the life we've built together,
for your steadiness and your love.

-

for my parents,
thank you for the love that raised me,
and the foundation that made all of this possible.

this book is my way of holding on,
of remembering what it felt like to be here,
in this life, in these moments -
so I wrote it down,
hoping I could keep it, even just a little longer.

this life, in all its fullness and fragility,
is the greatest gift I will ever know.